# WAVE INTO WAVE LIGHT INTO LIGHT

## POEMS AND PLACES

GEORGE H. NORTHRUP

# WAVE INTO WAVE LIGHT INTO LIGHT

POEMS AND PLACES

GEORGE H. NORTHRUP

International Psychoanalytic Books (IPBooks)
New York • IPBooks.net

Copyright © 2019 George H. Northrup and IPBooks

International Psychoanalytic Books (IPBooks)
Queens, New York
Online at: www.IPBooks.net

All rights reserved. This book may not be reproduced, transmitted, or stored in whole or in part by any means, including graphic, electronic, or mechanical without the express permission of the publisher except in the case of brief quotations embodied in critical articles and reviews.

Book design by Dan Williams

ISBN: 978-1-7320533-2-8

Printed in the United States of America

# About the Author

GEORGE H. NORTHRUP, PH.D is a psychologist who lives and practices in New Hyde Park, New York.

He is the author of a chapbook of nature poems, *You Might Fall In*, published in 2014 by Local Gems Press. Other poems have been published in scores of journals and anthologies. Northrup has led the Fresh Meadows Poets (organized in 1986) since 2006, and for eight years served on the Board that selects the Nassau County Poet Laureate.

He has been in the private practice of psychotherapy since 1987 and for decades helped train clinical psychologists at St. John's University. Northrup emerged from the nearly cloistered chambers of the classroom and consulting room in 2009 to serve a term as President of the New York State Psychological Association, followed by three years on the Council of Representatives that governs the American Psychological Association.

# Contents

## Without the Oysters

3   Plantation
4   The Oysters of Oyster Bay
5   Sedona Experience
7   In a Bistro on the Left Bank, 1946
11  Indigestion in Isla Verde
12  First Presbyterian
13  Great Myths of Long Island
17  Hobnobbing with the Gods
18  Capitol Punishment
20  Niagara Falls
21  Newark Street Scene
22  Nature Morte: A "Still Life" en Français
23  Showdown in Forest Hills
24  Mounting and Dismounting
26  From the Neue Galerie through Central Park
27  Berkshire Footfalls
29  Middle Falls, Letchworth State Park
30  Once Around the Pond
31  National Museum of Rodin
32  Across the Tiber
33  From Fields Once Torn by War and Slaughter
34  San Gimignano: Manhattan of Tuscany

## Dawn's Dark Origin

39  Star Island, 4:00 a.m.
40  Turning 60 on a Winter Morning in Cape May
41  Mid-March at the New York Botanical Gardens

| | |
|---|---|
| 42 | Visions of the Genesee |
| 44 | Time Travel |
| 45 | Mt. Kailash |
| 47 | Saratoga Springs |
| 49 | Stellar Moments in the District of Columbia |
| 51 | Chicago: on the Bus, off the Bus |
| 53 | Gondola Mistress |
| 54 | In the Nest at Eagle Village |
| 55 | As Told Over a Cold Beer After Hiking Boynton Canyon Trail |
| 57 | Resisting the Romantic Impulse |
| 59 | Irish Snippets |
| 60 | Floruit |
| 61 | Riverside Park |
| 62 | Caught in the Radiance |
| 63 | Montauk Point |
| 65 | Beach Religion |
| 66 | Bienvenidos |
| 69 | What to Watch For |
| 70 | Stepping Out of Pinewood Lodge |
| 71 | Lost in the Seaview |
| 73 | Dawn at Yavapai Point |
| 75 | Radical Acceptance |

## Coda

| | |
|---|---|
| 79 | Ceramic Impressions |
| 80 | Acknowledgements |
| 82 | Notes |

# Introduction

LET NO ONE think of these poems as mine in any narrow sense. To be sure, I have labored over them, but when I stop to think of all those who helped shape the poetry into its present form, the authorship feels more like a collective. I thank especially George Wallace for the classes that inspired a number of these poems; the Fresh Meadows Poets, who are often the first audience for my work; the circle of relatives and friends who provide constructive feedback; and the gentle wisdom of Gladys Henderson, Elaine Preston, Muriel Harris Weinstein, Ginger Williams, and John Williams.

    I am also grateful to Alan Kazdin, who so often took time out of his busy life to offer compelling words of encouragement; to Henry Seiden, who combined vigorous editorial comments with a sincere willingness to let me ignore his suggestions; and to Christopher Bursk, who offered valuable edits of individual poems as well as crucial ideas about the organization of the book as a whole. Despite all this assistance, of course, the shortcomings are my own.

*June, 2017*

# Without the Oysters

## Plantation

Crowns of long leaf pines
titter uneasily in dawn's billowing breath.
Anoles scramble up the screen
covering the lanai. Anhingas—
or maybe cormorants—perch by the lagoon,
shrewdly distant from a young alligator
sunning himself. The tide is out,
exposing treacherous pluff mud
along the tabby sea wall.

Each unique home is nestled carefully
among loblollies and cabbage palms,
semi-occupied by wealthy refugees
escaping Northern winters.
The Property Owners' Association
prescribes the exact shades of paint
to be applied, even to mailboxes.
Other species may wear
whatever hides or feathers
they prefer, but humans shall not dress
in blue jeans at the Country Club.
For angels of this paradise,
the main activities are dog walking,
bicycle riding, aerobics, golf,
and the consumption of spirits.

## The Oysters of Oyster Bay

Land is worth too much
for forestry or farming now.
A lane is not a lane as once—
it is a long, hatched strip
of asphalt motorway.

Parks and preserves
commemorate nature's
obsolete uses.
A greenhouse stores efficiently
endangered specimens.

Back yard framed in fence
evokes a wider, greener space.
We *are* the world, we think,
and truly in this trim urbanity
our scent hangs everywhere.

Who has seen a possum or a wolf?
Who knows the languages of birds?
We have the place names
of indigenous people,
but not their hunting grounds.

We have Oyster Bay
without the oysters.

## Sedona Experience

Los Abrigados Inn
leaves a bottle of water
in the kitchenette
"for the thirst-quenching
convenience of our guests"
and warns that
"a charge of $6.00 will be added
to your bill upon opening."

Nearby a complimentary tea bag
is stapled to a bold reminder
that more are available
in the Resort Gift Shop.

Generous sizes of shampoo
and "maximum body conditioner"
greet the traveler
at the bathroom sink
with—yikes!—a "Special Offer"
to purchase these for $19.95.

On the coffee table lies
a brightly colored magazine,
*Experience Sedona*,
on every page
an opportunity to spend.
The Dining Experience,
The Lodging Experience,
and, of course,
The Shopping Experience.

Here, in red-rock country,
where the Chamber of Commerce
is said to rest upon a vortex

negative in qi,
where you cannot even
drive back from Safeway
without a mesmerizing view,
experience Sedona
while you can,
before they hang tall curtains
on the canyon walls
and charge your credit card to revel in
The Viewing Experience.

## In a Bistro on the Left Bank, 1946[1]

"Only two things matter in all the world,"
Jean-Paul begins, "the rest can fall away.
Only two things, love and jazz,
which are, after all, the same."

*Welcome to the hell of ideas,* thinks Simone,
while keeping a social face.
*Was that a jam session last night?*
*But no, you cannot keep the boys*

*from treating even mental constructs*
*as enticing objects for flirtation*
*and seduction, coaxing bashful thoughts*
*to ribald escapades.*

She had selected her largest earrings
in a calculated move,
hoping to suggest a long stride
out of the Jungian shadow.

"Except for existentialism, the entire contents
of the mind are delusory inventions,"
he continues, "solipsistic analgesics
for the ache of nothingness."

"True," notes Boris, "and how we long for
the vacuous helium of our bourgeois balloons
to lift us from the naked terror of a life
with no inherent meaning whatsoever."

*If I could deflate their balloons,* Simone imagines,
*they might descend to human rank again,*
*but would remain as blind and deaf*
*to sentient experiences and to me.*

"I write only for my own amusement,
and the world, uncomprehending,
adorns me with bohemian celebrity.
What could be more disgusting?"

"Even your disgust is manufactured,
Jean-Paul. The mental factory of nausea
is repelled by its own productions
and trapped in the very revulsion."

*If we must proceed in circles,* she reflects,
*why not one more voluptuous?*
*Revulsion is indeed a common trap;*
*the question, then, becomes*

*by what elusive means to find release.*
*In my silence I assert Desire*
*as authentic antidote to nausea*
*and basis for all existential choice.*

"Surely you would agree," Boris ventures,
"that the farce of transcendence
is the primary fabulist pitfall
of western intellectual thought?"

"Transcendence of what?
The pull to expatriate ourselves
from our stark phenomenology merely
substitutes one inauthentic being for another."

"Now you might have stumbled
onto something," she remarks aloud,
with a sly, triumphant look.
"Expatriate indeed!

*"Ζευ' Πατηρ! Pro patria mori! Paterfamilias!*
*A genealogy of smug paternalism*
*in its manifold and ugly forms,*
*which are, after all, the same.*

*"There is a crude, ancestral archetype*
*beneath your thought, which shapes*
*this dialogue unconsciously*
*because, as males, you cannot see*

*"the symbolic phallic contest in your repartee.*
*Language emerged in synchrony*
*with sharpened stones—both as tools*
*of penetration and of dominance.*

*"The outcomes may vary,*
*may even swell the arts and sciences,*
*but the hunt, Messieurs, is driven by*
*the frenzy of pinning the kill."*

"Very good, my dear Simone,"
Jean-Paul replies. "But who is not
a prisoner of his own essential nature?
Or *hers*, for that matter?

"Your charming tease is the necessary irritant
to rouse the male desire for engagement
with futility—you are the muse
in this absurd theater of dialogue."

"And so," Boris offers, "Inevitably we mistake
our conviction of being right
for what we call reality.
This could be our deepest flaw."

"All mental formulations, Boris, fail
as ontological communications,
less than the stutter of birdsong
or the hollow voice of thunder.

"Traditional philosophy is just another
chirp or clap, mere acoustic stimulation,
not even a more elegant waving of sound,
like Benny Goodman or Cab Calloway.

"Do we agree?"
"Let's continue tomorrow."
*Better than sex*, Boris thinks,
*or the same thing, after all.*

## Indigestion in Isla Verde

Puerto Rico

The lady at the next table
in Mi Casita (famous for mofongos)
elevates her voice above the din.
Because of a problem with the water main,
they gave her disposable tableware
instead of 'silver.'

"I simply cannot eat like this,"
she complains to her ancient husband,
and tells the server to pack up the food
when it's ready, but not
with any plastic forks and knives.

As she waits, I notice the toes
in her sandals begin to twitch.
"It's twenty minutes already,"
she announces to Methuselah,
who probably wishes he were listening to Vivaldi
or watching waves applaud the beach.
Like me, he wishes she could find
vacation somewhere in herself.

**First Presbyterian**

There it was, in Southampton,
commanding Main Street,
The Oldest Presbyterian Church in America,
its posture stiff and angular
in upright dignity,
pure white, by clear design.

The Oldest Presbyterian Church in America,
attended by
the oldest Presbyterians in America,
tight-lipped and thin,
well over a hundred,
somberly entering
and somberly returning
to the day's renunciations
and responsibilities.

They are long-lived because virtuous,
virtuous because never debauched
by those raucous Italians
carrying a life-size statue
on the feast of Saint Catherine of Sienna
in a baroque procession
with candles, incense, and song—
as if heaven were here on earth,
as if faith were a carnival.

## Great Myths of Long Island

In the beginning was Big Duck
drifting in the sky like a cloud
searching for a place to land.
And Big Duck saw marshes, ponds,
and broad beaches. He saw the ghosts
of Montauk and Matinecock tribes
and the white hills of clam shells
they had left behind.
As Big Duck flew over the Great City,
he saw soldiers home again from the world war,
living in crowded apartments.

A hundred years before,
Horace Greeley had said, "Go west, young man."
But Big Duck said to the people of the Great City,
"Go east." And the people scrambled into Levittown
and Massapequa, Nesconset, Oceanside,
Port Jefferson and Quogue, Ronkonkoma.
And soon they had backyard pools and barbeques
and lawnmowers. On weekends they were
painting the trim and planting azaleas
and it all seemed like a good idea.

And it was a better life, after all,
rid of cockroaches and landlords
and the screech of subway trains
and the fear of crime.
It was a good beginning, you could say.
It was a nice place to raise a family.
And Big Duck saw what he had done
and quacked.

But was it enough, after all?
Or was satisfaction a moving target,

a race one could not win
relaxing on the patio?
Slowly, the people embellished
what they had, expanded the house,
bought a sailboat and a second car,
a condo even further east,
where they could admire
each other's burnished tan.
And if they could not have these things
they dreamed of them.
And they had built a shrine to Big Duck
in Riverhead, but when it got in the way
they moved it to Hampton Bays.

They filled their kitchens with granite and stainless steel,
and their bathroom fixtures they adorned
with brushed nickel and antique brass.
They chopped bits of olive into their loaves,
bits of cranberry and walnut into their sausages.
They turned out their potato farms
in favor of Merlot and Cabernet.
They stopped raising ducks.
They devoured pizza topped with free range chicken
and broccoli rabe, washing it down
with boutique beer and designer water.
On special occasions they dined on surf and turf
followed by a chocolate mousse or crème brûlée.

And as they lay in bed sleepless,
they realized they had eaten well
but missed the celebration.
They were offended by the insularity
of their neighbors,
the narrow causes placed above community.

They feared their dreams were hollow,
their marriages expired.
They saw their children had been richly taught
that anything of value can be bought.
They thought of their Porsches
and their Jaguars, which they had,
and the open road, which they did not have.

Some of them remembered stickball
and Green Hornet and dancing to the Top 40
and soft ice cream on weekends in the summer.
They remembered having only one telephone,
one bathroom, one car, one dollar in their pocket.
They remembered sleeping well
and walking on stilts and jumping into piles of leaves
and neighborhood football games
and trick or treat before the fear of razor blades.

And they cursed Big Duck who had led them here.
They challenged him to swim in Long Island Sound
like a great feathered whale, where he might
stretch their imaginations to bigger thoughts.
Others wanted him to roast himself on a giant spit
in Nassau Coliseum, by this sacrifice
redeeming everything that had gone so wrong.

And Big Duck heard the clamor of the people
and he said unto them,
"I have given you the finest teachers,
graceful waves patiently instructing,
grains of sand so densely packed
but fitting perfectly together,
solemn pines that point both up and to each other.
But you have moved my shrine to Hampton Bays

and sent the little ducklings far away.
For this I have punished you with Canada geese
that refuse to leave your golf courses
and block the traffic on your streets.
But I am a merciful Duck and I forgive you.
And this I say unto you, 'Go east'."

As the people listened to the words of Big Duck,
they grew perplexed. And they said to him,
"We have gone east as far as we can.
If we venture east of Montauk or Orient Point
we will drown in the sea."

And Big Duck quacked.

## Hobnobbing with the Gods

The Waldorf-Astoria lobby floor
is finished like a Roman palace
in pixels of mosaic tile.
Potpourri freshens the restrooms,
fireplaces dignify the conference halls,
and velvet-covered handrails guide
the pampered palm to greater heights.

Staying here makes a man feel
like one of those Brand Name People
who leave their mark upon the world—
Captains of Industry commanding
legions of mercenaries,
Government Brass being polished in the spa,
Hall of Fame Athletes competing at the bar,
Cinema Legends posing as vérité,
and Literary Giants sneering at Lilliputians.

Their wives should be famous, too,
for putting up with them heroically.

## Capitol Punishment

By Holly wooed and Disney whirled,
535 trick-or-treaters, dressed as
senataurs and congressaurs and
shouting the pledge of a grievance,
fling into air the bright confetti of fiduciary scruple,
swarm up the Capitol steps like San Juan Hill,
swaying in a conga line,
lost in the beat of their bongos.

Five hundred thirty five incongruous
slack-jawed gargoyles (the finest money can buy)
doze through committee meetings,
dreaming their fondest dreams of white houses,
red states contending with blue.

At the twilight's last gleaming, lawyers and lobbyists
descend like paratroopers from on high,
singing of pork and perk and Patrick Henry—
Oh, how they sing!—some with a twang,
some with a honeyed, grandiloquent drawl.

Blinded by stars, by wavy stripes,
535 unindicted Congressional co-conspirators
seek to pin tales on donkeys and elephants
in the grand old game of kerfuffle.
A disconsolate chaplain beseeches any higher power
to release the mudslide of divine grace on those
who toil in the cloakrooms here below.

A Congress of 535 twittering leaves
on the legislative branch waves and bows
in the sultry Potomac breeze.
Amid the volley of bullet points
(bombast bursting in air)

they bellow *whereas* and *be it resolved,*
finding money needed today
in the abundant fortunes projected
for one fine day of reckoning.

Starbuckled and bespoken, a Congress
of 535 Lex Luthor look-alikes
parades a large, sticky ball of hoopla
down Constitution Avenue,
gathering whatsoever my fellow Americans
no moss (Por favor! No mas!)
and singing the national anathema
as Uncle Sam, stilted and flagged,
pitches new bonds to the free.

## Niagara Falls

Old taverns and repurposed brothels
in Niagara-on-the-Lake
bloom with canna and petunia flowers.
Here are souvenir shops—new, but looking quaint.
One is your falls, the other ours.

Mercantile will established portage routes,
finessed artillery around the falls
for eager forts to guard the shipping lane.
Unable now, as then, to hoard its wealth
Niagara freely spends its fluent showers.

Shrewd and dedicated engineers
have catalyzed this wasted thunder water
with commerce and electric power plants.
Casinos and balloon rides flourish.
Aloof above the falls: hotels' gigantic towers.

Here, in history, where cannons used to volley,
Rainbow Bridge binds bank to bank,
taunts the politics, the absent-minded folly
of any claim to ownership or boundary,
while fettered nature yields, but never cowers.

Blazing in the cloudless dawn
ascending sun inflames the wakeful hours,
sets all the molecules in motion,
kindles drastic antidotes
for man's ambitious powers.

**Newark Street Scene**

The young black fellow
crossing this sunny street
with me on the way to
the Performing Arts Center

is far more perceptive than I:
when a policeman directing traffic
in the intersection shouts,
"Hey, where are *you* going?"

I hardly hear his challenge.
To me he is background noise
not quite breaking through
my wall of privilege.

But the young man hears him.
Every corpuscle in him knows
he is the one being questioned.
He is far too socially aware

to show in his tactful reply
any trace of what is
surging through his blood,
tensing in his arms and legs.

## Nature Morte: A "Still Life" en Français

Paris Metro station Île de la Cité

Blond curls cascaded in a soft
baroque brocade across her neck,
suspended just above
the stiffened shoulders
in her trim black coat.
Stately and slender,
she carried like a scepter on her arm
a tall ensemble from the florist,
wrapped in paper
except for a blossom or two,
as hidden as herself.

When she turned around
to sit on the train,
I could see the young face:
how artfully formed,
but weary with a chronic care,
masking that with prim reserve—
imperious, the hint of a pout—
one face superimposed over another,
reciting a layered history.

Anorexia, I guessed,
and fear of that humiliation
known best to those so like herself,
whose wary glance falls
now and then on one
more shimmering than she.

## Showdown in Forest Hills

He strides, defiant, from the curb
against the light just changed.
Likewise pressed by time,
but given green permission,
I slowly drive ahead.

One block away I'm stopped again,
the signal red; like hailstones he appears,
berserk and banging on the window,
"Why don't you let people
cross the street, *ass*hole?"

Then, scraping a key across
my door and fender,
he takes the opportunity to add,
"And your stupid car
needs a paint job, *ass*hole."

*I am not like you*, each thinks,
this coarse antithesis of two.
No chance that *we* will soon
replace this self-important *I*,
that irritating *you*.

## Mounting and Dismounting

Lenox, Massachusetts

Marriage to bipolar Teddy Wharton
must have bolstered
Edith's need for symmetry
when she and Codman
made their blueprints for The Mount.

Rattled by his mood swings,
she trusted her own sanity
to the principles of classical design,
insisting on a window *here,*
even with a staircase crossing it,
because she'd placed one opposite,
*there* on the left of the façade.

The gallery required double doors,
but one end opened to his study,
where all the other doors were single—
*Work it out somehow, can you, Mr. Codman?*

The higher Teddy flew
and the deeper he sank,
the more grounded she struggled to be.
*None of that fussy Victorian gingerbread!*

Her gardens have a fountain at each end,
and she might have squared Laurel Lake
if she'd been able.
*Tell the dandelions not to root*
*except in rows or circles.*

In less than ten years
the marriage collapsed anyway.
She fled to Paris with her little dogs.

## From the Neue Galerie through Central Park

I inspected harbor prostitutes
and legless veterans in Weimar cabarets—
their suppurating blisters in merciless light.
Even these hideous portraits by Otto Dix
tutor the eye to see more vividly
the wilting red azaleas
in all their limp surrender.

His drug-dazed heroines, cruelly observed,
make more astonishing
the rise of rhododendron's lacy globes.
Are people truly that ugly and misshapen?
Are some trees more beautiful than others?

"I had to get it out of me," he often said,
as if describing pus or constipation.
There, the marble staircase
and the paneled chambers
guide perception, magnify the artistry.

Here, on a park bench, where a sudden gust
retrieves me from extended reverie,
afterimages of green—green everywhere—
soothe wounded eyes still wincing
from his gruesome study, all in red,
of young Anita Berber
on the fast track to death.

## Berkshire Footfalls

Younger maples populate
this soaring hillside amphitheater.
Here and there an ancient one stands out,
too big around for firewood,
not straight enough for lumber
when ax and saw were busy here
a century or more ago.

This birch tree leans directly out
of Robert Frost's familiar poem,
reaching down as if to touch its roots.
Where you see one, look around for more,
each bending from a heavy winter weight
the trunk remembers.

A vine as thick as any blacksmith's wrist
encircles this old maple,
rising seven stories up the trunk
in symbiotic, serpentine pursuit.
Branching near the ground, another vine
leaps straight upward fifty feet
before it fastens on the tree—
which can't be possible, but here it is,
like some logger's cable left behind.

The largest dandelions I have ever seen
decorate this unexpected clearing
where humid sun so thickly streams,
their stems tall as tulips,
blooms wide as silver dollars.

The heart could be this man-high
stub of trunk, so totem-like,
half chewed by grubs,
machine-gunned by woodpeckers,
and plastered with a dozen hives.
My pace accelerates, retreating now
downhill—the journey home unwinds
as something in the wind provokes a shiver.

## Middle Falls, Letchworth State Park

Finished quenching green thirsts of spring,
the Genesee River trickles through mid-summer,
carefully descending this great cliff
as if holding a wobbly handrail.
What surged and roared a season ago
ambles in diffidence now.

Much of its former sparkle has vanished
into the ground or into sunbeams,
though, even now, the flow is always
too much to cradle in his hands.
It courses on, carries itself gingerly
around obstinate boulders,
approaches bends with wary curiosity,
and sleeps in quiet pools,
as if conserving strength.

Watching the river's simple clarity—
transparent in substance and direction—
he stands with a faraway look,
imagining snow falling at dusk
and the stiffening passage into ice.

## Once Around the Pond

Gerry Pond, Roslyn, New York

These benches are as bare as tree limbs now—
summer lost, fall's bright colors fading gray,
the placid surface of the pond inscrutable,
where mallards swim, stranded in the dimming light.

He pictures vanished water lilies here,
hallucinates the missing butterflies.
Old pines loom spare and strangely indolent,
a few of them in shrouds of ivy gauze.

Dry reeds along the shore, forlorn and stiff,
will soon succumb to winter's slashing gusts.
Today's chill air constricts an aging duct,
from which a single, cautious tear descends.

Will nothing keep these raucous gulls away?
They stammer messages from sky and sea—
rude fanfare as a distant ambulance
approaches with its wailing siren song.

## National Museum of Rodin

So near alive they call for pity,
some of them huddled naked
in the Jardin de Varenne,
too proud to shiver
nor resenting the mud today;
some chopped at the neck
like counter-revolutionary men;
some half born, writhing
in birth canals of stone.

I—not made immortal by Rodin,
not cut from marble blocks
nor cast from bronze—
emerged between urine and feces,
living warm, dying soft in fragile skin.

## Across the Tiber

Castel Sant' Angelo

Mausoleum built for Hadrian,
then haven for the angels
of Farnese and Borgia
flying down the long Passetto.

Marble and bronze
were long since carried off
to serve the living, one of the
smaller Roman treacheries.

Now—bare bricks guard history.
Pigeons nest in niches
once imperial
lining the Hall of Urns.

Now—Monsignor Ambrosiano,
with his briefcase, hurries down
the Via della Conciliazione,
Mussolini's gift to the Pius.

## From Fields Once Torn by War and Slaughter

The same bounty of wheat emerges as before,
the same grapes and olives ripen,
the same cattle graze.
But war has reaped a generation from the living,
has sown the fields with shrapnel—
a legacy not pacified by fences,
by the rhythm of planting and harvest,
nor by this gentle autumn night
as the season cools.

A weary farmer marches
to his stone house by the road.
Behind his back a sentry sun
inspects the amber meadow—
appearing innocent of danger—
nourished by rain,
by vegetative rot, by cow dung,
by the blood of lost armies.

From fields that warn of war and slaughter
come cricket calls, a crow's complaint,
the whisper of a strolling wind—
and even now, just beyond earshot,
the hammering of fierce artillery,
men shouting in panic, enveloped by smoke.
In war's laconic aftermath, fallow voices mouth
a speechless armistice.

### San Gimignano: Manhattan of Tuscany

These gray medieval towers
do resemble modern office buildings
in their severe, squared-off design
and astonishing height.

But this is not midtown
or the financial district,
here on a Tuscan hilltop,
where history lies exposed,
speaking not from a page
but from the setting itself,
history thick as the summer air.

It speaks in the sinister curves
of these ancient, narrow streets,
in wind that carries still
the dying moans of dark-aged
victims of the plague.

The old cathedral's frescoes
prepared departing penitents
for gruesome judgment
falling sooner than expected.

History speaks from the stone towers,
stone houses, stone walls, stone streets—
each rock an answer to the fear
that prompted all this building:
a place meant never to yield,
as strong as man is not.

Through this gap,
a crossbow might be aimed.

From here, hot pitch hurled
down upon a hostile clan.

Tourists with gelato
flip through prints on sale,
take pictures at the well,
gawk at the torture racks
and iron maidens in the Devil's Tower.

In June sunlight and bustle of day
the chill of old terror recedes.
No bells mark the night watch.
Armies Siennese and Florentine
no longer rumble through the valley,
are safely bivouacked in time.
Cascades of jasmine vines
dangle from the walls, sweet subterfuge,
perfume to mask a pungent history.

Tour buses leave by dusk,
shops begin to close;
secrets of the old village
emerge as they have for 800 years.
Dark shadows animate the walls.
Villagers in coarse and simple cloth
prowl the maze of alleyways.

Here on this hilltop redoubt,
the vaunted safety of the place
conjures, evokes its opposite
as fiery stars above direct the eye
to a colder, greater darkness all around.

# Dawn's Dark Origin

**Star Island, 4:00 a.m.**

Tennis courts are empty,
fountains in the lagoon
stilled for the night.
Ducks are hidden away,
folded in sleep.  No music,
no children's games
disturb the quiet air.

This could be a postcard
of dawn's dark origin
captured at the moment
just before one
can possibly know
if the day
will be cloudy or clear.

## Turning 60 on a Winter Morning in Cape May

Awakened early by a gnawing curiosity,
I stand before the window with its partial ocean view,
observe the foaming waves that splash around the sandy
  brim.
A sunlit brilliancy conceals the record-setting chill.

This picture is the same in every season;
the waters move but mostly keep their place.
Is that the voice of gulls outside
or just a laundry wagon squeaking down the hall?

The sea is full of lies and full of answers—
people visit, posing questions, and accept
the sloppy hints and inchoate suggestions,
the mostly reassuring nods of simple waves.

Surely I have done the things that people ought to do,
have studied, worked, obtained a house, and loved,
have grown more satisfied and generous with age,
even kept a few things for a purpose all my own.

Predictable and steady, but with a storm or two,
the sea is stupid, lumbering, and slow,
or—peaceful, confident, and strong.
The waves are full of answers, full of lies.

## Mid-March at the New York Botanical Gardens

He is searching for signs of spring,
eager to greet the season's first bees,
nearly desperate for something green
after winter's hoary avalanches.

An orchid show consumes
the Enid Haupt Conservatory,
fun house for phalenopsis,
carousel of cattleya.
There is lady slipper bedlam
in this throng of paphiopedlum.

Dressed all in black, a somber esthete
stares into his viewfinder, hoping
to capture forever this filtered light,
this extravaganza of cymbidium.
A toddler screams,
pressing fingers to her gum,
where a tooth intends to bud.
A wizened crone bends closer
to inspect a prickly pear.

Not satisfied with these
exotic indoor specimens,
he heads outside to Wamsler Rock,
outcrop of gneiss and schist,
where he encounters
in a patch of bare earth
solid proof of early spring:
a single ragged crocus
torn by wind and rain.

## Visions of the Genesee

Letchworth State Park

I. Inspiration Point

Standing on this bluff
pitched far above the bed below,
I scarcely hear the river's
ceaseless scraping flow.

Stillness rises
from the settled motion here
as time collapses to a crawl
and nature's pace falls temperate and slow,
heavy with the tribute of springs and creeks
as far upstream as Pennsylvania.

To what depths, I wonder,
might this river make me go
if I could linger?
How much could it wash away?


II. Lower Falls

Two days of rain have filled with mud
this trail descending to the river bank.
The bustling, swollen water plunges
in a sudden angle to the stream,
flinging fine mist high into the air.
Soon the river narrows
and for a short distance
overfills its bed.

The woods hold dead
and wounded trees,
victims of an ice storm.
Old growth had long outlasted
such assaults,
needs time for slow decay,
while moss applies
a soothing poultice.
No one feels a stranger here
or out of place.


III. Wolf Creek

Beginning just above
the creek's own shy, sequestered falls,
an unmarked path ascends among the pines
to a panorama of the Genesee,
its soaring canyon walls
topped by turkey buzzards, four in all,
coasting through the air
on warm updrafts,
waiting for something to die.

Cliffs so near the sky,
the stream of time so deeply underfoot.
From the buzzards
to the river down below,
the eyes in sweeping motion
ride a vast, hypnotic pendulum.
What speaks is utterly hushed.
What thinks eludes conception.
And what falls into the ages—pauses here—
glad for a place like this.

## Time Travel

It is November in Queens,
but the morning sun in my eyes
reminds me of summers long ago
traipsing through Baja,
free as a pelican gliding
over lazy waves,
thin clouds a wispy veil
before a baby blue,
unformulated future.

It is November, and I am driving
to a windowless classroom
in the university basement,
introducing my students
to the agile mind of empathy—
assisted today by dolphins,
by tequila, by love's first memory
playing its oboe on a sunlit beach.

## Mt. Kailash

It is always cold here, cold and forbidding,
slippery snow and icy rock,
Himalayan air as dry and thin as death—
all part of the warning to be
as desperate for enlightenment
as a man with his hair on fire
is desperate for a pond into which to jump.
Otherwise, don't begin!

Here ponds are frozen, and the jump is astral.

Up and up from Lake Manasarovar,
climbing through exhaustion
on this seabed coral lifted to the sky,
Kailash wielding wisdom's hammer
far above my stubborn skull.

Here at the top of the world,
still and barren,
here at the top of the world's emptiness,
age-old truth is post-Newtonian:
nobody connected to nobody.
Only the connection is real.

Now the clouds are thickening;
we can scarcely see each other.
I would vanish *if not for the tie to these others,*
here in freezing nights, disoriented days—
Shakyamuni, trekmates, Sherpas,
even the Chinese border guards—
*if not for the tie to these others*
circling the sacred mountain
together.

Here physics reigns in radiance
with metaphysics, uniting local and cosmic.
Within these soaring, iridescent peaks
ions and eons empty into present fullness,
not found on any map.

Say this without words, Kailash,
looming in pantomime.
Say it in stony silence
so everyone can hear.

## Saratoga Springs

Yet another head cold dims the neural circuitry,
makes ruddy health a fog-filled memory,
and isolated cases of swine flu
still dominate the television news.

Trees are late to bud this year;
I should be grateful for the evergreens.
Tired feet reluctantly accept
the virtue of a stroll from my hotel.

I discover the Automobile Museum;
its fleet of hundred-year-old cars
invokes the era of my father's childhood.
I wear his ring for company today.

He once described that fateful day
his father drove back to the farm
steering the family's first car, a Model T,
and no one knew, as they approached the barn,

how one might bring this carriage to a stop.
Grandpa pulled back firmly on the wheel,
commanding, "Whoa!" to those steel Clydesdales
straining, sweating underneath the hood.

I meet a wealthy old collector from
Caracas, who pays a curator
to oversee his forty-two superb antiques,
each perfectly restored, like new,

each still a jaunty presence on the road:
Pierce-Arrow, Stanley, Metz, Peugeot, and Benz.
Locating molds to cast spare parts
is not so difficult, he says.

At the ticket counter I had almost
veered from that young man with hearing aids,
prism spectacles, and asymmetric face,
welcoming and offering directions.

I notice him again when exiting.
Familiar now, he offers me,
"A pleasant evening, sir!" as sunset nears.
Smiling back, I trundle through the door.

## Stellar Moments in the District of Columbia

Red Shift on the Red Line

The two girls, each about sixteen
and obviously lit from deep within,
did not careen or slur their words,
but what else could have made them,

so late on a handsome Friday night,
accidentally start to climb
the broken ten-story escalator
in the Metro at DuPont Circle?

A gray-haired man motioned them
toward the working escalator
just several feet away for a more—
as he said—*uplifting* experience.

They shone more brightly in the long ascent,
as he fell backwards through his life,
old boy dropping all seniority
until he reached sixteen, himself.

What did they chatter on the way?
The lyrics hardly matter,
only the pulsing of the beat,
the crackle of celestial heat.

When their maiden incandescence
reached the zenith of the stairs,
they beamed him a bright good-bye,
and the constellation of their legs

dimmed in the enveloping night.
As he stood transfixed and stranded
on the chilly, darkened street,
they flickered in the distance.

## Chicago: on the Bus, off the Bus

Both of us waited at the bus stop
late on Saturday night.
He—maybe twenty, in jeans,
unshaven and thin;
I—three times his age, in a business suit,
bearded and plump.
We boarded together in silence.
He seemed to be napping for awhile,
head in his hands
on the back of a seat rail.

And then I felt his hand
on my shoulder
"What bus is this?" he asked.
*The Number Three.*

"Where does it go?"
*Well, I'm from out of town,
but it goes north on Michigan Avenue.*
He thanked me, made a phone call
that I couldn't overhear.

"Where are we now?"
*About 400 North Michigan Avenue.*
Preparing to step off,
he turned to face me.
"Thanks, man, for being so nice."
*That's OK, you're welcome.*
"You know, you could have been
an asshole, but you weren't.
So, thanks again."
*It's really all right.
I was young once, too.*

He still looked grateful
as he staggered out,
but eyed me quizzically,
searching for some vestige
of that other youth
once tripping through the night
and looking for direction.

## Gondola Mistress

Until the Doges reign again in palaces of pink,
until the silk route sings again
of proud Venetian fleets,
gondola mistress of the liquid labyrinth,
we shall prolong this old affair.

For now, the Queen of the Adriatic
sinks below her knees.
She hides decay with crimson,
puts new paint on cracked foundations.
Now polished jewels distract from tired flesh.
Time rumbles in a plaintive basso continuo.
We feel our age, gondola mistress,
but do not mind going along for the ride.

Assured by time of your appeal,
you will not heave or slide away
from under me, I know,
if my eyes investigate other supine carriers
primped and displayed for eager gentlemen.
They would be women of the streets
if there were streets.

You have retained your curves.
Your slippery bottom wiggles willingly
as I, your gondolier,
inhale your musky scent and
murmur our favorite tunes
above the lapping waves.
I ask no more than transport,
no more than gliding up
and down this Grand Canal.

## In the Nest at Eagle Village

Bushkill Falls, Pennsylvania

On every day but one of our vacation
plainsong showers chanted
softly through the pines.
The many hours spent indoors
on this, our first extended trip
together in five years,
collapsed the wary distance we had kept
to calm the daily friction.

Once you gave yourself a chance,
you liked this place you'd first refused—
cathedral ceilings in the major rooms,
a private deck to view the lake,
a little herd of white-tailed deer
approaching on the lawn.

My arm felt right again
around your shoulder,
bodies softer now and older.

You never cared for slapstick,
but as I watched that classic movie,
*It's a Mad, Mad, Mad, Mad World,*
I laughed so much you almost
joined me in the pure hilarity.

## As Told Over a Cold Beer after Hiking Boynton Canyon Trail

Sedona, Arizona

The guide book said the trail was moderate,
whether moderately easy or moderately strenuous
was left ambiguous.  It pegged the "elevation rise"
at just four hundred feet, meaning,
as I came to understand, eight hundred down
and twelve hundred up, and down and up again.

All the bees in Arizona were holding a convention
in a field of flowering manzanita,
through which the trail itself
looped like the flight of a bee.
And the sun was so hot
halfway there I tried to drink my hat.

I climbed over rocks and tree roots
and over a few collapsed hikers, too.
Deep in the woods, a coyote studied me
the way one reads nutrition labels in the market.
So I grabbed a nearby rattlesnake, lassoed his neck,
and tied that puppy's legs together, like in a rodeo.

The climb grew nearly vertical,
hand over hand, foot over foot, foot over hand
crabwise up the canyon wall.
"Is it much farther?" I began to ask
other hikers on their way back down.
"Yes," they all replied, but I persisted.

And it was worth the blisters,
prickly pear thorns, and the sunburn
just to see the canyon's head,
its craggy pulpit and limestone choir loft
patiently waiting a few million years
for a congregation to gather.

## Resisting the Romantic Impulse

*For Henry Seiden*

Clear aesthetic standards
forbid me to write a poem entitled,
"Walking Through Rainbows at Bushkill Falls,"
even if that is exactly what happened.
It would sound contrived and sentimental,
wishful thinking mixed with fairy dust,
Wordsworth on psilocybin.
I would have to begin with "Oh!" or "Lo!"
to warn the reader of a grand pathetic ecstasy.

It had started with a sleepless watch
last night as slashing wind
and torrents from the Caribbean Sea
poured half a foot of rain
on the Pocono Mountains—flooding Route 209,
tossing limbs against electric power lines
in Pike and Monroe Counties,
sending every gully brook and freshet
scurrying downhill to Bushkill Creek.

Even the willing suspension of disbelief
requires a semblance of truth
with which to infuse the fantastic.
This densely-bowered, grueling hike
from Lower Bridesmaid Falls
(over every slippery rock and gnarled tree root
a soggy earth could set beneath my feet)
might be allowed in post-modern verse.
But not this bright surprise of bliss
at the foot of the Main Falls,

where a deluge fell with such exuberance
it sprang back up the canyon walls,
fine prismatic droplets
bending afternoon sunlight just so,
blinding me with rainbows (three, I think).

A poem like that would have to end
in giddy dissolution, this I know,
as the improbable narrator
standing on a wooden footbridge
no longer could distinguish
his own heavy perspiration
from the cool spray of the falls
that kissed him everywhere—
he taken in by it all, taking everything in,
happily surrendering
any cogent distinction whatsoever
between himself and a rainbow.

## Irish Snippets

"We enjoyed a splendid summer—the rain was *warm*."

Some crows of Quin
in raucous chorus
circle over horses,
cattle, sheep,
who feast on thirty seven
shades of green.

Two faiths,
two languages,
two favored drinks:
a pint of Guinness
at the Brazen Head,
a pot of tea at Bewley's.

## Floruit

"*Did* he flourish? When?"
one might inquire
with a skeptical toss
of the head.

*Precisely now*
(though his dates
are still approximate),
here on the Grand Central Parkway
speeding through Queens
to a poetry reading
as blue and gold celestial acrobats
cavort in open air.

Then, on to the Bronx.
He has his folding bicycle
in the trunk,
plans to ride the streets
of City Island (our Île de la Cité),
has the *Times*, Mozart,
books, an appetite for fish,
a ticket to the Botanical Gardens.

His foot on the accelerator,
flying, flying like the wind
up the Rota da Luz.[2]

*Floor it.*

## Riverside Park

Under leaves that hold like prisms
final smiles of a horizontal sun,
comes a chilling thought to scold,
presaging the distemper
of endless cloudy days:
I should be writing that report,
buttoned into bankers' grays,
a noose of silk,
growing rich instead of tan.

The winter will be on
and in me soon—
I would not deny
the year its weather—
but I have won this afternoon,
still young,
tickled by a feather
of a breeze,
kissed by the sun's gold tongue.

## Caught in the Radiance

Jones Beach

My desk is covered with important papers,
some of them waiting since the last millennium.
My list of chores in the computer
gathers gigabytes.

On such a glossy afternoon,
my ambitious academic friend
is probably finishing his latest book.
I'm here at the beach, catching photons,
playing hide and seek
with ultraviolet light,
listening to gull gossip,
playing chicken with the surf.

A broad blue banner draws the eye
above horizon's hazy brown;
distant waves cradle the gaze
before their final somersault in sandy foam—
my little portions of oblivious beyond.

A child in geography would wonder,
"Why do they give them different names—
oceans, seas, and bays?
Don't they know it's all connected?"
Maybe they were just
naming the parts, like finger,
knee and foot.  I like that better
as I squander afternoon
on what may be the last
perfect beach day of the season,
turning wave into wave,
light into light.

## Montauk Point

At first it resembles an eating contest,
each devouring another:
oyster drill sucking its prey,
thirsty ticks engorged with doe and fawn,
men with the catch of the day,
a rough sea swallowing whalers
and lobstermen
remembered here in stone.

Waves, in dedicated friction,
grind old rocks to sand
and would do the same for me.
Immolating sun swelters and churns.
How curious to find in all this anarchy
here at the last outpost of land
such a rhythmic, comforting repose.

Consider how far this wave
has dragged its gown
to curtsy here before the Hither Hills.
Above, a flaming sun to grill
and, steps away, a syncopating surf
to chill my empty hide—
salt sweat to salty sea
I'm finding here.

As soon as we are busy,
the cadence of the moment breaks away.
Not knowing this, or forgetting,
lifeguard blows his whistle,
mother shouts at Christopher,
and a dune buggy growls
down the beach,
restoring place and time.

If they distract me,
I have lost the mystic rhythm;
annoyed by my distraction
I have lost again.
Re-finding follows this reminding:
they also beam and wave,
who in their different forms,
incarnate pulsing harmony.

Pink of morning, pillow winds—
here the old Atlantic
snuggles with the sound,
the bashful, silent sound.
All the gravity of earth
has pinned me to this sunny place,
this littoral truth.
Two breezes waltz
upon the Walking Dunes.

## Beach Religion

Porpoise Cove

Yellow-footed snowy egrets
stand in clusters at the beach,
accepting with no hesitation

two great egret cousins
whose feet are black,
and us, the human population.

Sun is burning through
the morning haze.
We talk of Zen and life riparian,

how to cherish, not to cling.
Buddhist too, she calls herself
a hyphenated Unitarian.

## Bienvenidos

Newark, New Jersey

Although I never emigrated,
I live in a foreign country now
because the longer I live
the more novelty I encounter.

I cannot name the popular singers
and actors in this unaccustomed country,
not even many of the news commentators.
Novelty is all around me, from Frankenfood
to the arcana of übersmart devices.

Foreign is not what a baby would call
its blooming, buzzing confusion,
though everything is new to the baby.
Foreign is what's new to someone
who already has experience in life.

Sometimes life is baby-new to me,
as when I tried to walk through a glass wall
at the Sheraton this morning.
I'm a tourist from another era, another world,
marveling in this strange parking garage
at all the poured cement columns
that look like gigantic golf tees.
The parking spaces squares on a chess board,
my Toyota in the bishop's place.

In new experiences like this
I could try to reassure myself, *Oh yes,
we have something like that at home.*
Like déjà vu—half recognized, half new.

I am foreign even to myself,
breaking into unexpected futures,
altering my appearance,
scattering the ashes of past lives,
and starting old age
with the latest virgin of the same wife.

I live in a foreign country now—
I suppose I always did.
In this unfamiliar deli,
when I order a medium coffee to go,
the Latino man behind the counter
asks me something in an accent
so thick I cannot understand.
I wish I were fluent in Spanish.
Next time I will know what he means,
except that next time he will be
someone from Ghana, Vietnam, or Kerala.

*Welcome*, I say, to all of us.
*Welcome to this foreign country,*
not an English colony anymore,
not even the melting pot they taught in civics.

That metaphor implied too much assimilation.
We are more like cau-cau or sambar,
Masamam Curry or Chicken Zharkovia—
exotic stews in which some flavors
blend and some remain distinct.

I know this, I believe it, even if
every national chauvinism,
every patriotic protocol
dictates that new arrivals are the ones

who should accommodate.

Now I would be satisfied to recognize
a portion of myself, here and there,
gamely floating in the sauce,
picking up some unfamiliar flavors
while adding a little body to the dish.

## What to Watch For

Driving up the switchbacks
in Oak Creek Canyon
he sees a sign that says,
"Watch for Rocks,"
and he wonders
if it means *in the road*
or *tumbling down the cliffs*.

Except for the clear blue
Arizona sky
and some evergreens
he can't tell apart
at this distance,
rocks are about all
one can watch for.

Gazing at rocks
is why people come to Sedona.
They come from Moscow,
New York, and Tokyo
to stare in amazement.

As his eyes engage
the hulking, rugged view,
he imagines other signs
inviting travelers
to "Watch for Four-leaf Pinyons"
or "Watch for Bright Sunshine"
(in the road
or tumbling down the cliffs).

## Stepping Out of Pinewood Lodge

Castile, New York

Pine trees persist
in pointing at the stars
even as daylight's eraser begins
wiping their tiny sparkle from the sky.

Birds sing matins to each other,
And a lusty breeze gropes everything
on this hilltop, scurries away in search
of more sleepy darlings to caress.

Look at this artful waterfall,
flirting with cliché,
performing without audience
in misty darkness.

Chipmunks and other monks
tread without aim
in the same perfection,
finishing one moment,

seamlessly starting the next,
alive in present fascination
for as long as it lasts,
as long as it takes.

## Lost in the Seaview

Galloway, New Jersey

Each of the sleek but
unobtrusive chrome nozzles
of the hotel's sprinkler system
taps a hidden pipeline
branching back to larger
and still larger conduits,
then outside to a water main
buried under the street.
A nearly infinite regression
carries the mind upstream
to a distant lake or reservoir
and, from there, perhaps,
even to the clouds.

This morning's breakfast egg
sits on my plate
in deceptive isolation
from the cook, grocer,
truck driver, hen, farmer,
and all who nurture them
and all of their ancestors—
too much to fit on a plate.

"Look both ways before crossing the street,"
we say, alert to those dangers,
but who warns against following
the lengthwise trajectory of road,
its vast synaptic connections
branching out as far as Juneau
and Tierra del Fuego?

Consider the telephone: we talk to it;
someone hears us far away
through copper, fiberglass, or air.
Our closest model might be prayer.

## Dawn at Yavapai Point

Grand Canyon, Arizona

A shy first light inspects the ancient stone;
spiny buttes and plunging cliffs
entice the drifting mist.
Rabbit brush is flowering now.
A chipmunk on the rim
shivers in the morning chill,
shivers in the quickening.
Above, a raven glides.
Juniper and cypress spice the air.
Here is a presence thick with past—
desert to sea and desert again,
wind chiseled, water worn,
a billion days to sculpt.

The foot, self conscious, inches near.
Below—a hazy vision of Bright Angel Trail.
From the edge of nothing, brink of naught,
the eye, transfixed, adores
the distance and the depth.
Here opens to infinity,
more than sense can receive.
Hozho.[3]
Wait for the bloom of agave.[4]

*Spürest du*
*Kaum einen Hauch.*[5]
Wind and amber sun,
snowmelt and sandstone,
deliver us from the chatter of ourselves.
*Die Vögelein schweigen im Walde.*[6]
Deliver us from the rattle of ourselves
in reckless motion.

*Warte nur, balde.*[7]
Draw deeper from its lofty perch
this mischief mind.
Follow the Abyss to Hermit's Rest.
Find me a simple bunk
below, at Phantom Ranch.
*Ruhest du auch.*[8]

## Radical Acceptance

Everything happens just as it should,
August perspiration stinging my eyes
during the long wait for an express bus
and, of course, this sluggish queue of traffic
approaching the Midtown Tunnel.
Even the potholes make perfect sense.

Everything is exactly right—
like this sudden downpour
as I drag my suitcase
from the bus to Penn Station.
The broken escalator—have no doubt—
fulfills a noble purpose.

This horde of tourists on the stairs,
stopping every few steps
to look around in wonder,
does not so much block my path
as point me to a better way,
only seconds till departure time.

A benign universe delays
the occasional train.  All is in order,
all is well—my aching plantar fascia,
the brevity of gratitude,
even the elusive mind of acceptance,
everything just as it should be.

# Coda

## Ceramic Impressions

Whenever I travel, I bring home
a coffee cup as souvenir,
so every morning,
still wandering from sleep,
I select a destination to revisit:
Sistine Chapel, Golden Gate,
the Hall of Mirrors at Versailles,
or Bunratty Castle, by the Shannon estuary.

On Hilton Head, a thrift shop
sold me a pair of cow-painted cups.
They remind me of the Gullah culture
slowly buried under condominiums
and of my family's long-forsaken farms
in the hills of western New York.

Some of my oldest cups—
from Big Sur and Manchester, Vermont—
are far more perfect than my recollection,
while others—hand-crafted by a
peyote-inspired artist near the Grand Canyon
or bearing the subway grid of London—
have collected chips,
sharp wounds to brittle memory.

Gone is the delicate china cup
commemorating Queen Elizabeth's
fifty years on the throne,
which I dropped for only an instant
but shattered forever.

# Acknowledgments

*American Society: What Poets See* (anthology): "Sedona Experience"

*Axis of Logic:* "Capitol Punishment"

*Bards Annual:* "Nature Morte: A 'Still Life' en Français" and "Niagara Falls"

*Crossing the River: an Anthology in Honor of Sacred Journeys:* "Mt. Kailash"

*Freshet*: "Ceramic Impressions," "In the Nest at Eagle Village," "Floruit," "Gondola Mistress," "Indigestion in Isla Verde," "San Gimignano: Manhattan of Tuscany," and "Saratoga Springs"

*Long Island Quarterly*: "First Presbyterian" and "Montauk Point"

*Möbius: The Poetry Magazine*: "From Fields Once Torn by War and Slaughter"

*Nassau County Poet Laureate Society Review:* "Newark Street Scene"

*The New York Times* Metropolitan Diary: "Hobnobbing with the Gods," "Radical Acceptance," and "Riverside Park"

*Of Sun and Sand* (anthology): "Beach Religion"

*Performance Poets Association Literary Review*: "The Oysters of Oyster Bay" and "Turning 60 on a Winter Morning in Cape May"

*Sproutonlinemagazine,* "Caught in the Radiance"

*StepAway Magazine,* "Chicago: on the Bus, off the Bus"

*String Poet:* "What to Watch For"

*Toward Forgiveness* (anthology): "Showdown in Forest Hills"

*Writing Outside the Lines* (anthology): "Great Myths of Long Island"

# Notes

[1] Inspired by a picture of Jean-Paul Sartre, Boris Vian, and Simone de Beauvoir in *The New Yorker* dated December 25, 2006 and January 1, 2007, which is, after all, the same issue.

[2] (Portuguese) The route of light.

[3] (Navaho) "Harmony" or "walking in beauty."

[4] A cactus with very sharp pointed leaves, sometimes called "the cowboy killer." It was at first thought to bloom only once in a hundred years.

[5] You feel scarcely a breath. These and the following lines are from a 1780 poem by Goethe, "Wanderers Nachtlied II."

[6] The birds are silent in the woods.

[7] Just wait, soon.

[8] You, too, will rest.

www.ingramcontent.com/pod-product-compliance
Lightning Source LLC
Chambersburg PA
CBHW052110070526
44584CB00017B/2419